# ENDANGERED LEOPARDS

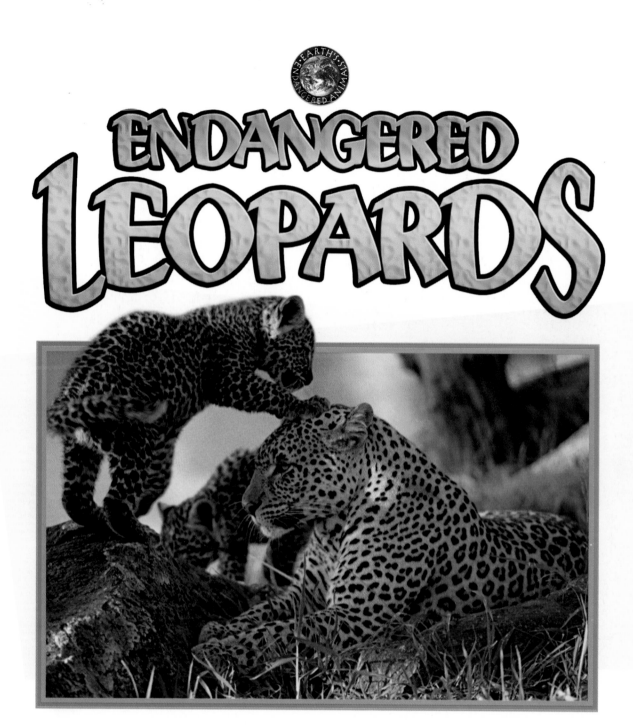

## Bobbie Kalman & Hadley Dyer

Crabtree Publishing Company

www.crabtreebooks.com

# Earth's Endangered Animals Series
## A Bobbie Kalman Book

Dedicated by Mary Learn
To WWF for their dedication in protecting our wildlife

**Editor-in-Chief**
Bobbie Kalman

**Writing team**
Bobbie Kalman
Hadley Dyer

**Substantive editor**
Niki Walker

**Project editors**
Kristina Lundblad
Kathryn Smithyman

**Editors**
Molly Aloian
Robin Johnson
Kelley MacAulay

**Design**
Margaret Amy Reiach

**Cover design and series logo**
Samantha Crabtree

**Production coordinator**
Katherine Kantor

**Photo research**
Crystal Foxton

**Consultant**
Patricia Loesche, Ph.D., Animal Behavior Program,
Department of Psychology, University of Washington

**Illustrations**
Barbara Bedell: pages 5, 6 (lion and tiger), 15, 16, 29, 31
Tammy Everts: page 30
Margaret Amy Reiach: page 6 (cat)

**Photographs**
ardea.com: John Daniels: page 8 (bottom)
Keith Levit Photography/Index Stock: page 18
Naturepl.com: Richard Du Toit: page 25;
 Fabio Liverani: pages 22-23;
 Anup Shah: page 17
NHPA: Martin Harvey: page 27 (bottom);
 Andy Rouse: page 9 (top)
Photo Researchers, Inc.: T. Kitchin/V. Hurst: page 10 (bottom)
Visuals Unlimited: Wendy Dennis: page 28
Other images by Corel, Creatas, Digital Stock, and Digital Vision

## Crabtree Publishing Company

www.crabtreebooks.com          1-800-387-7650

**Cataloging-in-Publication Data**
Kalman, Bobbie.
 Endangered leopards / Bobbie Kalman & Hadley Dyer.
  p. cm. -- (Earth's endangered animals series)
 Includes index.
 ISBN-13: 978-0-7787-1856-7 (RLB)
 ISBN-10: 0-7787-1856-5 (RLB)
 ISBN-13: 978-0-7787-1902-1 (pbk.)
 ISBN-10: 0-7787-1902-2 (pbk.)
 1. Leopard--Juvenile literature. 2. Endangered species--Juvenile
literature. I. Dyer, Hadley. II. Title.
 QL737.C23K343 2005
 599.75'54168--dc22
                                          2005000346
                                              LC

**Published in
the United States**
PMB16A
350 Fifth Ave.
Suite 3308
New York, NY
10118

**Published
in Canada**
616 Welland Ave.,
St. Catharines, Ontario
Canada
L2M 5V6

**Published in the
United Kingdom**
73 Lime Walk
Headington
Oxford
OX3 7AD
United Kingdom

**Published
in Australia**
386 Mt. Alexander Rd.,
Ascot Vale (Melbourne)
VIC 3032

# Contents

# Le⊚pards are endangered

Leopards are **endangered** animals. Thousands of other **species**, or types, of animals are also endangered. Without help, endangered animals may become **extinct** within a few years. Keep reading to learn more about leopards, why they are endangered, and what people can do to help them.

4

## Words to know

Scientists use certain words to describe animals in danger. Some of these words are listed below.

**vulnerable** Describes animals that may soon become endangered

**endangered** Describes animals that are in danger of dying out in the **wild**

**critically endangered** Describes animals that are at high risk of dying out in the wild

**extinct** Describes animals that have died out or that have not been seen in the wild for at least 50 years

# What are leopards?

Leopards are **mammals**. Mammals are **warm-blooded** animals. Their bodies stay about the same temperatures, even when the temperatures of their surroundings change.

Mammals have backbones inside their bodies. Baby mammals **nurse**, or drink milk from the bodies of their mothers. Most mammals have fur or hair on their bodies.

## The cat family

Leopards are part of the cat family, *Felidae.* Other members of the cat family include lions, tigers, lynxes, and bobcats. **Domestic**, or pet, cats are also related to leopards.

domestic cat

lion

tiger

6

*This mother leopard is watching over her babies as they nurse.*

# Eight kinds of leopards

*Most Amur leopards live in a part of Russia called Siberia. Some Amur leopards live in North Korea and China.*

There are eight **subspecies**, or kinds, of leopards. Anatolian leopards, North Persian leopards, South Arabian leopards, Amur leopards, Javan leopards, North Chinese leopards, and Sri Lankan leopards live in different parts of Asia. North African leopards live in Africa. These eight subspecies are known as "true leopards."

## Critically endangered!

All leopards are endangered, but some leopards are critically endangered. Anatolian, Amur, North African, and South Arabian leopards are all critically endangered.

*North Persian leopards are the largest leopards. They live in Iran, Afghanistan, and Turkmenistan. These countries are in Asia.*

8

*Sri Lankan leopards live on the island of Sri Lanka, which is near India. The tails of Sri Lankan leopards are longer than are the tails of other leopards.*

## Not leopards

Snow leopards and clouded leopards are called "leopards," but they are not true leopards. In fact, these animals are not closely related to true leopards.

*Snow leopards live in mountainous areas in Asia. They are endangered animals.*

*Clouded leopards live in rain forests in Asia. These animals are vulnerable.*

9

# Leopard homes

The natural place where an animal lives is called its **habitat**. Leopards live in many habitats, including forests, rain forests, deserts, **savannas**, and on mountains. Some leopards live in warm **climates**, and others live in cold climates.

*Leopards that live in dry places, such as savannas or deserts, can go a long time without drinking water. They get the water they need from the food they eat.*

*Leopards that live in cold climates have longer and thicker fur than do leopards that live in warm climates. Thick fur helps keep leopards warm in cold climates.*

## Alone on the range

Adult leopards are **solitary**. Solitary animals live alone. Each leopard has a **home range**, or a territory in which it lives. Although leopards often share parts of their home ranges, they try to avoid one another.

## How big?

In areas where there is plenty of food, leopard home ranges can be as small as a few square miles. Leopards that live in rain forests, for example, do not have to travel far to find food. In areas where food is hard to find, home ranges are much larger.

*The home ranges of most male leopards are larger than the home ranges of female leopards. The bodies of male leopards are bigger than those of females, so males must eat more food.*

11

# A leopard's body

Leopards are known for their beautiful spotted fur. Their fur can be light cream to dark gold in color, depending on where the animals live. The fur of leopards that live in rain forests is darker than the fur of leopards that live in grasslands or deserts. Light fur helps the leopards that live in grasslands or deserts blend in with the golden colors of their habitats.

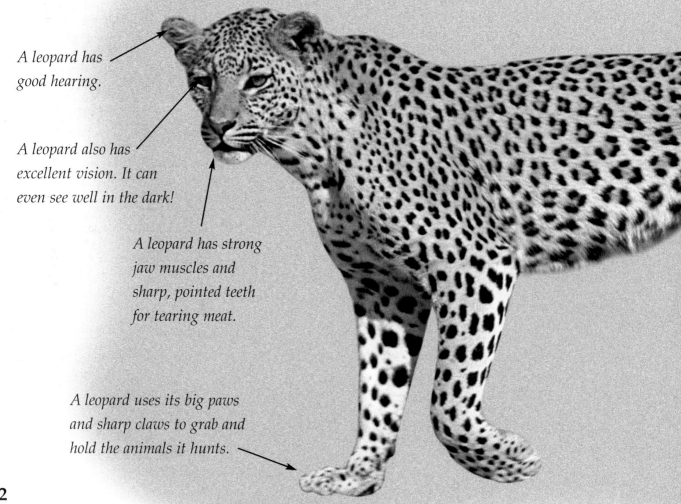

*A leopard has good hearing.*

*A leopard also has excellent vision. It can even see well in the dark!*

*A leopard has strong jaw muscles and sharp, pointed teeth for tearing meat.*

*A leopard uses its big paws and sharp claws to grab and hold the animals it hunts.*

12

## Built for hunting

Leopards have sleek, powerful bodies that are built for hunting. Leopards are fast runners. They can run at speeds of up to 36 miles per hour (58 km/h). Leopards can also leap long distances and jump high into the air. They are excellent climbers and swimmers, as well.

*A leopard's tail is almost as long as its body. Having a long tail helps a leopard keep its balance as it runs and makes sharp turns.*

### Black leopards

Some leopards have black fur. Black leopards have spots, but their spots are hard to see. Many people mistakenly call black leopards "panthers."

# Finding food

Leopards are **predators**. Predators are animals that hunt and eat other animals. Animals hunted by predators are called **prey**. A leopard's prey includes monkeys, warthogs, large birds, and snakes. The leopard usually **stalks** its prey until it is close enough to pounce on the prey. After pouncing, the leopard grabs its prey with its front claws and bites the prey's neck.

*Most leopards are **nocturnal**. Nocturnal animals are active mainly at night. This leopard has killed a baboon.*

## Out of reach

Lions and hyenas often try to steal prey from leopards, but leopards protect their prey. They drag their food high up into trees, where lions and hyenas cannot reach it. Leopards can carry animals that are larger than they are! They often leave their prey in the trees for days and return to eat it whenever they are hungry.

# A leopard's life cycle

Every animal goes through a set of changes called a **life cycle** as it grows up. A leopard begins its life cycle when it is born. It grows and changes until it is **mature**.

A mature animal is an adult. Adult leopards can **mate**, or join together with other adult leopards to make babies. Each time a **cub**, or baby leopard, is born, a new life cycle begins.

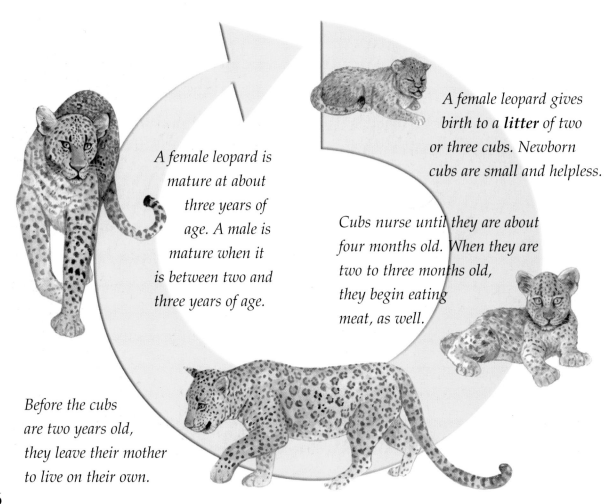

*A female leopard is mature at about three years of age. A male is mature when it is between two and three years of age.*

*A female leopard gives birth to a **litter** of two or three cubs. Newborn cubs are small and helpless.*

*Cubs nurse until they are about four months old. When they are two to three months old, they begin eating meat, as well.*

*Before the cubs are two years old, they leave their mother to live on their own.*

16

## A safe place for cubs

When a female leopard is ready to give birth, she finds a safe spot to make a **den**. A den is a hidden shelter. After giving birth, she keeps her cubs in the den for about eight weeks. Living in a den helps the cubs stay safe from predators.

## Growing up

After leaving the den, cubs learn to hunt by playing. They chase one another and other small animals. Cubs pounce on almost anything that is smaller than they are! When cubs are about three months old, they join their mother to hunt larger animals.

*Cubs catch small prey such as mice, turtles, and hares. This cub has caught a hare.*

# On their own

Before they are two years old, most leopards leave their mothers to find their own home ranges. As adults, leopards get together with other leopards only to mate. Leopards fight if they meet one another at any other time.

## Keep out!

Leopards **patrol**, or keep watch over, the edges of their home ranges. They mark the boundaries of their home ranges to warn other leopards to stay away. They make their marks by **urinating** on trees and **shredding**, or cutting into, tree bark with their claws.

*This leopard shreds a tree's bark so that other leopards will see the marks and stay away.*

18

## Mating

When a female leopard is ready to mate, she gives off a **scent**, or smell. She rubs her body on the trees in her home range to leave her scent on them. When a male leopard smells the scent on the trees, he knows that the female in that range is ready to mate. The female also makes sounds to let the males know she wants to mate. After mating, male and female leopards do not stay together for very long.

# Less room for leopards

One of the biggest threats to leopards is **habitat loss**. Habitat loss is the destruction of the natural places where animals live and find food. People destroy the homes of leopards by **clearing** forests and other leopard habitats. When people clear land, they remove all the trees and other plants from it. People clear land to build farms, roads, and towns.

## Hungry leopards

Many plant-eating animals are prey for leopards. When land is cleared, the plant-eating animals that live on that land do not have enough to eat, and they soon die. Fewer prey animals means that the leopards have trouble finding enough food to eat in their home ranges. As a result, many leopards may starve, as well.

### Going to town

Hungry leopards sometimes search for food on farms and in villages, towns, and cities. Some people who are afraid of leopards kill them. Farmers often kill leopards to protect their **livestock**. They shoot the leopards or poison the food that leopards leave in trees.

# Hunting leopards

There are laws against hunting endangered animals such as leopards. **Poachers** are people who hunt these animals **illegally**. They kill many leopards each year for their fur, bones, whiskers, and meat. They sell the furs to people who make fur coats from them. Some people believe that the bones and whiskers of leopards can heal sick people, so medicines are made from these body parts.

## Sold in secret

It is against the law to sell or trade leopard body parts, but people still do it because they can earn a lot of money. In some areas, people can make more money selling a single leopard **pelt** than the money they could earn working at another job for a year!

*It takes up to seven leopard pelts to make just one fur coat.*

# Safe places

To help protect leopards, the governments of
many countries have turned leopard habitats
into **preserves**. Preserves are large areas of land
that are protected by governments. They provide
safe places for leopards and many other animals
to roam, hunt, and raise their young.

*Scientists visit preserves, too. At preserves, they can study leopards in their natural habitats.*

## Patrolling parks

**Rangers** are people who patrol preserves. They keep track of the animals, help any animals that are sick or hurt, and try to protect them from poachers. Preserves are large open spaces, however, so rangers have a hard time keeping out the many poachers. Once the poachers get into the preserves, it is easy for them to hide from the rangers.

## Safaris

At preserves, tourists can see leopards and other animals living in their natural habitats. The tourists shown above are on a **safari** to watch animals in the wild. Some of the money tourists pay for safaris helps maintain the preserves. Safaris also create jobs for local people, which encourages them to protect the leopards.

25

# Leopards in captivity

Many leopards live in **captivity**. Animals in captivity are cared for by people. Some captive leopards live in zoos, and some live in **sanctuaries**. A sanctuary is a place where people house and care for sick or injured animals. Sanctuaries also provide homes for animals that have been kept as pets. It is illegal to keep leopards as pets, but some people still do. Both zoos and sanctuaries offer people chances to see leopards up close and to learn more about them.

*Most captive leopards lead safe and healthy lives. Some leopards live for up to 20 years in captivity. The lives of leopards in captivity are very different from the lives of leopards in the wild, however.*

## Breeding leopards

Some zoos have programs for **breeding** leopards. They bring together males and females to mate. Breeding programs allow leopards to raise their cubs in safe environments. Since most leopards have only two or three cubs at a time, it is important that every cub survives. Each cub that grows up to be an adult can also mate and have more cubs. When more cubs are born, the leopard **population** increases. Population is the total number of one type of animal living in a certain area.

## Cub-sitting

People who work at zoos help mother leopards care for their cubs. They sometimes feed cubs with bottles to make sure the babies grow up to be healthy.

*Leopard cubs can get sore bellies after they eat. A gentle belly rub from a caretaker can solve the problem!*

# People helping leopards

Many people are working to help leopards survive. Researchers study leopards to learn more about how leopards behave, how much space they need, and how many leopards live in certain areas. Researchers also try to learn how old and how healthy leopards in an area are.

## Tracking leopards

Some researchers keep track of leopards by putting radio collars on them. The collars send out signals that let researchers know where the leopards are and how far they travel.

*This leopard has been drugged so a radio collar could be put around its neck. The collar will help researchers keep track of the leopard.*

## Helping at home

Many researchers involve local people in their work with leopards. They teach people who live near leopard habitats why it is important to protect leopards. The researchers want to help the local people live safely alongside leopards.

## How you can help

The best way for you to help leopards is to learn about them and their habitats. Spread the word about dangers to leopards. The more people know and care about leopards, the better the chances are that leopards will survive.

# Spot the leopard!

The spots on a leopard's fur are called **rosettes**. A leopard's rosettes are shown left. Some people confuse leopards with jaguars, which are other cats with spotted fur. Jaguar rosettes have dots in the centers, whereas leopard rosettes do not. Cheetahs are cats that do not have rosettes on their fur. Instead, they have solid black spots. Guess which of these three cats is the leopard.

## Which cat is the leopard?

*If you guessed that the cat in the middle is a leopard, you were right!*
*The cat on the left is a cheetah. The cat on the right is a jaguar. Well done!*

## Leopards online

To learn more about leopards and other endangered animals, you can visit your local library or go online. These websites will get you started.

- **www.nationalgeographic.com/coloringbook/leopards.html**
Print a picture of a leopard and color it!

- **www.pbs.org/wnet/nature/leopards/index.html**
Visit this site to see a video called "Leopards of Yala."

- **www.worldwildlife.org**
Learn about endangered species from World Wildlife Fund.

# Glossary

**Note**: Boldfaced words that are defined in the text may not appear in the glossary.

**breeding** Bringing together a male and a female animal of the same kind so that they can mate

**captivity** A state of being in an enclosed area, such as a zoo

**climate** The long-term weather conditions in an area, including temperature, rainfall, and wind

**illegally** Carried out against the law

**litter** A group of baby animals born to one mother at the same time

**livestock** Farm animals, such as cattle or horses

**pelt** The skin of an animal

**prey** An animal that is hunted and eaten by another animal

**safari** A trip during which people watch animals in the wild

**savanna** A broad, flat grassland found in warm parts of the world

**stalk** To sneak up on something

**urinating** Releasing waste fluid from the body

**wild** The natural places where animals live

# Index

1 2 3 4 5 6 7 8 9 0  Printed in the U.S.A.  4 3 2 1 0 9 8 7 6 5